Are You Tough Enough

A Fight Worth Winning

By Angela Lee-Easter

Pictures by Angela Lee-Easter

Lee-Easter.
Are You Tough Enough: A Fight Worth Winning

Unless otherwise noted, all biblical passages referenced are
from The Holy Bible, Authorized King James Version ®. *The
New King James Bible: New Testament and Psalms*, (Thomas
Nelson, Inc, 1994)

https://www.facebook.com/identifyingthebrokenpieces/
angela.lee.easter@gmail.com
yourdestinyproductions2017@gmail.com
http://angelaleemoody.wixsite.com/destinyproductions

Available at
amazon

<u>Acknowledgements</u>

I would like to thank everyone for their encouragement and prayers as I traveled this road of questions, seeking, and finally answers. Each one of you was an inspiration in your own way. I believe God places people in our lives for various reasons. Those reasons may not be obvious in the beginning, but eventually, we realize that their presence in our lives where part of our journey.

<u>Dedication</u>

Rodney Darrell Easter, my husband

Joydan, Shafia, Ranesja, Rodney Jr., and Jeremiah, my children

Nevaeh and DeWayne, my grandchildren

Table of Content
Your First Ministry

A Strong Ministry

Prologue

In this life, we will be confronted with many challenges. Although we may not want others to know our struggles, it does not negate the fact that they exist. As much as we may want to escape, there is nowhere to hide. As much as we want to pretend that the hurts and pains are just a figment of our imaginations, we feel the blows with every swing. No matter how strong we may think we are there is always a giant bigger than the one before. There is a question that we must ask ourselves each time a new challenge come; are you strong enough, to handle this new level.

The only way to identify your true strength is with the tools found in the Word of God. Faith (Heb.11:1) is a measuring tool that you can apply to the giant of doubt. The Race (Eccl. 9:11) is a measuring tool that you can apply to your endurance. The Fig Tree (Matt. 21:18-21) is a measuring tool that you can apply to your production. Most importantly, love (1 Corn. 13:8) is the measuring tool you can apply to your dedication. There are many measuring tools in the Bible, but unfortunately, they are not utilized as often as they should.

A fight worth winning is a fight that holds great value for the winner. What are you fighting for and is the reward worth the effort? No one beats against the wind, looking for it to surrender. Is your fight in vain? We are warriors, we never give up, because we know, we do not fight alone. The fight is fixed.

Our Heavenly Father has given us access to the enemy's camp, and we are aware of his strategy. We serve a God that has ordained our conquests; therefore, we never have to shrink back. We are tough enough because He lives in us.

Are you Tough Enough?

Are you tough enough? This is a question that every woman and man of God must ask. There will come times in the life of believers when they will begin to ask for more. They will desire a greater move concerning their spiritual level, their relationships, and even their occupational positions. Although, this is very normal as it relates to growth and development. However, the question remains, are you tough enough? Fights and struggles will be encountered when such requests are granted. To be perfectly honest conflicts will arise even when the desire emerges.

If you are to be a spiritual leader, enter into a committed relationship, or receive a promotion, it will require greater strength. When Moses, considered the things he had to face as a result of his desires, he considered the conflicts involved. The more desired, the more required. He struggled with self-doubt,

1

a disobedient and rebellious people, and a Pharaoh with a god mentality. Sampson, the strongest man in the world, even he wanted more; specifically, a companion, but he encountered many struggles along the way, to acquire the thing he desired. Elijah wanted Elisha's anointing, and along with that promotion, he gained his pains and his enemies, which accompanies such power.

As children of God, you will always desire a greater level, but with each level, you will fight a greater devil. Therefore, Christians cannot afford to be weak. You must be strong in the Lord and in the power of His might. His strength is made perfect in weaknesses. He has the power to keep you. You are powerless without him. ***Are you tough enough?***

Can God trust you with His power? Can you stay humble when promoted? Yes, you can do it! It does not matter what it sounds like, what it looks like, or what it feels like. It does not even matter what people may say about it. You will be able to accomplish and do great things in the name of Jesus. You are a Christian, which makes you a powerful individual. You are a soul winner, a disciple maker, a kingdom builder, a demon slayer, and an overcomer. You are a winner!

However, if you for one moment begin to trust in your abilities, you will fail. Trusting in your own strength is something you cannot afford to do. You must rely on God's promises to provide you with the tools you need to win. Yes, you are tough enough, because the greater one lives in you. Greater is He that is in you than he that is in the world. He wants to use you for the Kingdom. Therefore, everything you need he has in his power to release. He has made you tough enough to step into your purpose. Will you accept the challenge?

Mission Is Possible

Do not doubt your mission. God has orchestrated each step you will take.
The Mighty General is assigning your duties. Your strategic orders are set up for you to win and take over the enemy's camp. Your mission is possible because the Commanding Officer has all things working for your good. You must put on the whole Armor of God and fight the good fight of faith. The fight is fixed, and you are guaranteed to come out with the victory. Remember all things are possible for him that believes. Do you trust God to lead you to your expected end?

This World's system is opposed to God's Truth

Man's Truth	**God's Truth**
Mission Impossible	*Mission Is Possible*
Believe What's Seen	*Faith Comes by Hearing*
Conditional Love	*Increase and abound in love*
The Walking Dead	*The Living Dead*
Payback	*Forgiveness*

- *Love: Beareth all things, believeth all things, hopeth all things, endureth all things. (I Corinthians 13:7)*
- *Now if we be dead with Christ, we believe that we shall also live with him (Roman 6:8)*
- *Jesus said unto him if thou canst believe, all things are possible to him that believeth. (Mark 9:23)*

What a man believes to be a success, will fail in the end, but love never fails; love gives hope to the impossible? On this mission, we must see pass what is in front of us. Our vision must stretch beyond the natural. We must see the God, written vision on the wall. *(Daniel 5)* We must understand and embrace his instructions as we apply them to our lives. Obedience to the plan makes the mission possible.

Can you see it? God has stationed his troops in the mountain high above their enemies; we shall descend to the valley with a mighty strike. This attack will come as a surprise to the enemy because we abide under the shadow of God's wing. We are the Lord's mighty people, and our victory is ordained.

Your mission is possible. Preach His word
soldier, lay hands on the sick soldier, and cast
out demons for your labor is not in vain,
complete the mission. It is time to fight!

(I Do) Don't Stop at the Altar

I do, are two special words that can last a lifetime. There has to be an unbreakable commitment to keep them intact. When you say, I do, what are you saying, and to what are you committing? This small statement is a personal affirmation. When you say I do, you are publicly affirming the things you vow to do in the marriage. These two words form a profound statement. The statement does not just apply to the parties involved, it involves God as well. Now let us consider the power behind the statement. The vows are exchanged, and then, I do's, are stated, but often there is little or no understanding concerning the power behind, the I do's. Their power does not cease but they are continual.

The vows are exchanged and then, I do's, activates the power to seal and hold the marriage, as the couple's hearts makes its' declaration with a kiss.

The vows were never intended to stop at the altar or the ceremony. *What God has ordained, He will maintain.* Your vows are to God as much as they are to each other. When vows are broken, divine judgment is released. (Judges 3:8) *And the people of Israel did what was evil in the sight of the LORD. They forgot the LORD their God and served the Baals and the Asheroth. Therefore, the anger of the LORD was kindled against Israel, and he sold them into the hand of Cushan-rishathaim king of Mesopotamia. And the people of Israel served Cushan-rishathaim eight years.* (ESV) God does not take any vows made to him lightly. (Ecclesiastic 5:4) *When thou vowest a vow unto God, defer not to pay it; for he hath no pleasure in fools: pay that which thou hast vowed.*

Some vows were never mentioned at the altar. These unspoken vows have the power to strengthen the marriage as time passes. Are you tough enough to deal with the new issues that will surface in the marriage that will require new vows? These issues were not apparent during the ceremony, reception, or the honeymoon. Well, new encounters will require, additional I do's.

Remember, your I do's, goes far beyond the vows made at the altar.

Both individuals must understand that I do, vows them to share the responsibilities of their spouse's previous commitments, such as financial obligations acquired before the marriage, even caring for a child from a former relationship, or even allowing a sick or disable mother-in-law to move in.

I do, is also a vow that will cause acceptance of silence, even when much could be said. You are willing to allow your spouse to win a battle of words, to avoid conflicts. You will find yourself listening to boring activities of the day even when sleep is much more exciting. Many I do's, will be encountered during your union, and if your vows were true at the altar, they would continue to show truth throughout the union.

Unless otherwise noted, all biblical referenced are from The Holy Bible, Authorized King James Version ®. The New King James Bible: New Testament and Psalms, (Thomas Nelson, Inc, 1994)

After the Honeymoon

Personally, this experience has truly been eye-opening and life-changing for me. I imagine many newlyweds expect the honey to keep on flowing after the honeymoon. Unfortunately, the no flow is a shocking upset to new marriages. Nevertheless, I must let you know that the honey is still available; however, the continuous flow is up to you. If you want the sweetness to stay present in the union, it will require work. Honey does not produce mysteriously on its own; there has to be effort involved in the process of production.

When you take into account the insect's world, honey is produced by worker bees; if there are no bees and no work, there will be no honey. As the bees go from flower to flower, collecting nectar, they return to the hive with sweetness to complete what they have started. Within a marriage, this process must be repeated to add sweetness. A sweet marriage will require all parties to be

11

involved. A good marriage can grow to greatness as the individuals learn to add to what they have and in doing so; it will enable them to share their success with others. When honey is produced, it is collected and shared. If your marriage is producing honey, it will cause others to experience, its sweetness. A healthy marriage can heal hurting marriages.

Just remember when collecting honey there is a very good chance of getting stung. Hard times will come, disagreements will happen, and anger will be unavoidable. Keeping things sweet will not always be easy, but the results will be worth all the effort. After, the honeymoon things can continue to stay sweet, when intentional efforts are put forth.

My husband and I, work hard together to keep things sweet, although we both have very busy lives; we have an understanding that marriage requires each of us to be self-motivated. We have to motivate ourselves to attend to each other. Attention to detail is key, to a successful marriage. We have struggles, and we find it hard sometimes to find sweetness, but because of preexisting sweetness, we can stand during hardness.

Unexpected attacks are the reasons it is so important to add on to what already exists. Because, when it is needed there will be a limitless supply. Seeking ways to please each other, even in times when there is neglect is important. Remember, neglect will not be frequent and most times not intentional. However, self-denial is paramount, so stop seeking an instant return; love is unconditional. Your display of affection may not be reciprocated immediately, but it will return in time and on time.

If your honey is recognized as a priceless commodity, your marriage will not suffer lack in the area of sweetness. It is not a one-woman's or one-man's show. It will take the dedication and intentional applications of each party. Having the right mind concerning marriage will be an important factor in maintaining a healthy relationship. Good marriages stand the tests of time and grow from their lessons. If the tests and trials cause you to buckle under the weight of the preparation, the marriage will suffer injury. Working together is the heart of standing, as the stronger partner builds up, the weaker.

My husband realizes I have weaknesses; many of those weaknesses did not reveal themselves during the honeymoon stage. They begin to be exposed as a result of disagreements, likes, and dislikes. However, because he understood that everyone has their own cross to bear and their crown to wear, he took the good with the bad. I had to accept the same revelation, concerning him. We are different in many ways, but we have the same goal, and that is to please God and to fulfill his plan for our marriage.

Your Honey Collection Must Include

Communication   Compassion   Consideration
Closeness   Correction

As the Bride of Christ, we must communicate with God in prayer to understand how to love one another. When we show compassion and are sensitive in the relationship, it will build trust and a lasting connection. Consideration will demonstrate unselfish intentions, which will result in a more open relationship. Having a close relationship is not something that unfolds overnight; it will take work and patience as you apply the necessary ingredients. Your honey must have the right ingredients to produce the right results. Sometimes, corrections will be hard to swallow, but there must be trust in your partnership and in your heavenly Father, to ensure a positive response. Couples must never allow the outside to wedge its way between what you have built. Your ingredients may not be identical to others or mine. However, with trial and error, you will know what it takes to make your marriage great and what keeps the honey flowing.

What God Ordained, He Will Maintain

Do you truly believe that God ordained your marriage? If you are not married, do you believe that your relationship is part of God's plan and it will result in a Holy Matrimony? If you can respond with a yes to either question, then why do you worry about the rest? If God has ordained your union, then he will maintain it. Do you concern yourself with past or present failures? Fortunately, for you neither matters. God is in full control of your steps. If your union has been ordained, then the path that you are to walk has also been ordained. Now, if you spend time worrying about; will it last, does he or she really loves me, or am I strong enough, you will create chaos in the union. **<u>Your only requirement is to believe God.</u>** He wants the marriage to be an instrument that he can use. Your doubting is an interruption. You will cause delays that stand in the way of progress. God cannot operate in doubt.

If you are fully convinced that God is ordering the steps in your marriage or your relationship, you must trust him entirely. Your communication with him is vital. You must have communion with him often to acquire the necessary instructions concerning your life. If you were to tell me that God was speaking and had permitted you to proceed, but you had no prayer life, I would say, proceed with caution. To be certain about God's direction for your life you must stay in prayer, as an individual, and as a team.

Although, past hurts and disappointments will cause you to doubt, remember God wants you to put those things behind you and press toward the mark for the prize of a higher calling. He is able to keep what you commit to him.

Testimony Break
I am a Survivor

I have been there. I have done that. Matter of fact, I have a T-Shirt and a mug to prove it. I have believed God for many things. However, it was hard for me to believe that there could be a real man out there, someone who would stick around, and not abandon me. I was so familiar with men not staying. My dad left my mom, my grandfather was unfaithful to my grandmother, and I have seen and experienced abusive, lying, and unfaithful men all my life. The marriages that I have seen in my family were nothing to be desired. Therefore, why would it be different for me?

My first marriage was in 1993; it lasted twelve long years. It was a horrific train crash from beginning to end. After such a crushing experience, I tried again in 2008; I knew this was the one, the man of my dreams. I was convinced, he was a God sent. I was ready to walk in ministry with this supposed man of God. The night of our marriage, I found myself alone. Although he did come back, his actions that night would be an example of what the marriage would be like for the next seven years.

What a heartbreak! I do not think I have ever hurt so badly. I was devastated. I became a shell of the woman that I once was. I was lost in a dark and broken world. Although I held on to my God, my faith was shattered. I had to hold on to what pieces remained, to survive, the pain.

Sadly, I had been under the impression that my trust was in God all those years. However, I was under the influence of my own intoxication. Intoxicated with a longing to be loved and protected, unlike what I had seen in my lifetime. Instead of God leading, I was making choices, believing it was Him. He had not ordained it; therefore, he was not going to maintain it. Nonetheless, with his loving arms of compassion, he picked me up, dusted me off, and restored my hope in relationships, and I survived.

I've Turned My Last Cheek

The Word of God makes it clear to the believers in Matthew 5:38-40, that we should turn the other cheek. However, what do we do after that? The last cheek has been offered, and the slaps and punches are still coming. Well, some may say keep allowing it, for persecution's sake, while others may beg to differ.

If the scripture says to turn the other cheek and you have done so, maybe you need to offer something else. It is clear that this scripture is an indication for promoting peace. You have no more cheeks, but you do have time. Give an ear rather than retaliation. Work on the situation instead of retribution. God desires that we live in peace with all men. Learning how to maintain a climate that is void of hostility requires a Godly nature. Whether on the job, in your marriage, or social communications, Godly character is needed. Not to say, that you should be a pushover, but a physical response should

21

never be the first response. We are ambassadors of Christ, therefore; kindness, gentleness, and patience should be demonstrated during situations that involve conflict.

A peaceful response may be considered as an act of weakness or fear. To win the lost, we have to be different. We cannot respond as the natural man would. How can we possibly lead a lost and dying world if our lives are identical to theirs? This is why God says to the married, husband love your wives and wives love your own husbands. The Marital union represents Christ and his Bride, and they should never respond to each other harshly, but in love. It is the job of the Church to demonstrate love and not hate. We must not allow our fleshly desires to respond to heated situations.

Testimony Break
Jellybean Fight

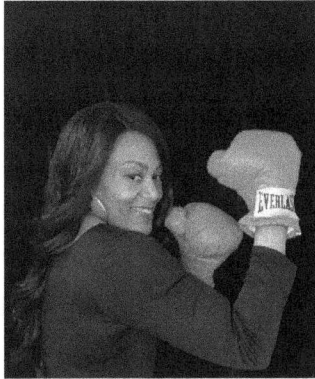

I am not perfect! I remember out of the very few arguments Rodney, and I have ever had, this one was most memorable. I call this one the *Jellybean Fight.* We had not been married very long, but one thing I recognized early in our relationship was our love for sweets. One day Rodney left his bag of jellybeans beside the recliner, in our office. I decided to watch my favorite show while eating his jellybeans. I did not eat the entire bag, but I had my fill. After, I was done; watching TV, I went to bed and did not give it another thought.

The next day was Sunday. As he was getting ready for church, he shook the bag, and boy, did it start. I thought it was somewhat funny at first, but later it escalated into a full blown-out word battle. I promise you I did not turn the other cheek; I was fired up.

After we both were extremely exhausted mentally and physically from the Jellybean fight, we calmed down and begin to unfold what happened. In our marriage, the resolution has always been the focus during our quarrels, as conflicts are not something we often experience. As a result, this time we both learned a valuable lesson. First, never allow the enemy to make a mountain out of your molehill. Second, step away from the Jelly Beans, sister.

We strive to keep peace and not allow Satan to wedge between us. The love we share does not allow for separation because separation is a result of unresolved conflicts. We had to find a way to put the fire out. The next morning, we both were very quiet (embarrassed). As we were locking up our home, preparing to leave for work, he called my name, "Angie." I turned around, he got

out of his car, walked up the steps, and
wrapped his arms around me so passionately,
and said, what I assumed every woman wants
to hear. His voice and his words put out the
fire and cleared away the smoke, that conflicts
tend to leave behind. He is such a humble
and loving man.

That day I bought him a peace offering,
which was in the form of two big bags of
Jellybeans, and as you may have already
figured it out, the issue was not really about
the Jellybeans. We realized once again how
crafty the enemy could be. He will use
anything to distract us from our assignment.
The war was bitter, but the peace treaty was
SWEET.

If Words Could Kill, I Would Be Dead

As I live and breathe, I would have never imagined the deep-rooted hate people could have for one another. However, it never ends with hate alone; it never ends until death is the conclusion. The death may not be physical, but definitely an end to how your righteousness is a constant offense to them. Since your life causes them to perform self-evaluations, they react in retaliation. They indirectly share your former failures and misfortunes with others to cover their faults and sins.

They send subliminal messages that inflict pain like small daggers, piercing your heart repeatedly. Their words are the very weapons of mass destruction with the intentions of ripping you apart. Many may ask, why allow their words so much power? Well, the answer to that question is; your love for them gives access.

I was in this position before I realized how to love people from a distance. Their words had the power to kill my spirit, cause depression, and inflict scars that were very difficult to cover. Fortunately, I found it hard for them to do any of these things from a distance.

I am reminded of the old saying; sticks and stones may break my bones, but words will never hurt me. I soon realized that this saying was not true. Words have the power to hurt and break. Words can break up good relationships; words can hurt and damage an already broken heart. Words have power.

However, the distance will keep the mouths away. Distance will identify your control over whom you allow power. It may be hard at first because it could be a close relative or a former friend. It could be your mother, who makes you doubt your abilities. In some instances, the distance may not be an option, therefore; you will have to learn to work under pressure. It may be your very own child, which constantly tells you that you are the worst parent ever, and he or she hates you. Sadly, enough it could be your husband or wife's words that choke the life out of you, and you see death as an easy escape, from the pain of their words. You are not alone. We all have faced similar pains. Remember, such things are just your training ground, it will not last, but your reactions to their words will never be forgotten.

I want you to know that words may come from someone you love. But you have to see the truth of the matter; God has greatness planned for you and Satan sees your future success. He is using those closest to you to prevent your moving in the direction of your destiny. Do not allow the words to kill, but allow them to push you closer to your goals. Sometimes the best place to be, is distant. This can be gained in various forms, time in Mount Sinai, time in the Garden of Gethsemane, or time in your secret closet. God has often removed his servants from family to complete their mission.

Rejection hurts, hateful words hurt, and false accusations hurt, ask Jesus, he experienced them all. Nonetheless, he had a mission and stuck to the plan. You too have a mission. Do not allow the devil to distract you with words. If words are killing you, then use your words to heal. There is life and death in the power of your tongue, speak life and live beyond words.

Killing Me Softly

It is true words can hurt no matter who is speaking. But when it relates to relationships the daggers used are not always apparent. To be honest, their appearance is far from that of a dagger. When words are spoken harshly in relationships, they are very damaging. Couples have to be careful not to allow irreversible harm to their union as a result of temporary tantrums. During the tantrums, words are often exchanged that are later regretted. These exchanges are done in the heat of the moment. They will usually cause unforgiveness and retaliation.

Sudden death to a relationship can be the result of words. It may not be a direct attack. Nevertheless, the sting is just as painful. In a marriage, both parties must be careful regarding what they say and how it is said. Words can eat like canker and remember canker grows gradually; it will eat away at the love in the marriage. If love is to grow and produce a healthy marriage, the husband and wife must be on the same page.

Please do not use hidden messages to get your point across, but with grace and love allow the Holy Spirit to season your words and communicate your position. Satan hates the marital union; he will use whatever tactics he can conjure up to break the bonds of love. His tactics are not obvious, he is very crafty, and if you are not careful, you will be caught in the grips of his destruction. You can lose it all focusing on his distractions. Your love must be tough enough to stand the tests of time.

If what you are facing in the relationship is killing you softly, then you are dying slowly, and before you know it, your union will be broken. Do not allow Satan to have your **Marriage!**

Going Back to Basics
First Lady Eve

Whenever we leave the basics of God's plan, we will encounter major consequences. If we want to experience the promises of God as he intended, we must go back to the basics. Too many times, we find ourselves complaining and griping because of where we are in our lives. We often say that we are not where we planned to be. We do not have the type of relationships we anticipated, we thought we would be married by now, our children are not what we thought they would be, nor are they doing what we thought they would do. We also have many thoughts concerning where we are and what prevents us from reaching our goals.

I must tell you, that a lot of what you are thinking can be traced back to the basics. I guess you are saying to yourself, Angie what do you mean by all of this? Well, my purpose for this book is to take you back to the basics. In Genesis chapter one, is where you will find the basics. Let us pay close attention to the first three Words of the following verses:

- Genesis 1:1 In the Beginning: (Basics)
- Genesis 1-3, 6, 9, 11, 14, 20, 24, 26, 29 (And God Said, And God Called)

I want you to think about these verses and consider God's divine order.

- Genesis 2: Who is talking? God and Man, they spent time together talking in the garden. God talks to the man about the garden and what was off limits.
- Genesis 2: Who did the work? God created it all, he did the work.

After God gave him the rules of the garden, he considered his lonely state. God said, in Genesis 2:18, it is not good for man to be alone.

At this point, many often conclude that God created the woman.

Well the Bible says, in Genesis 2:19, and out of the ground the Lord formed every beast of the field and every fowl of the air; and brought them unto Adam to see what he would call them. Genesis 2:20, for the first time mentioned, Adam speaks. I hope you are getting this; he is allowed to speak outside of his communion with God, as it relates to naming the animals. Now, why is he naming animals? (Because it is not good for him to be alone) Well, when Adam completes naming the animals, he realized in Genesis 2:20, there was no help meet found among the animals.

Christian brothers must understand that before the right one comes; the animals will come first. If you can identify the animals, you will have the power to recognize a good thing, a wife. Adam recognized the animals, named and identified them, realizing none of them was for him. Although some animals are beautiful, strong, and dependable, they are still animals. You must Wait for your First Lady.

When Eve, was created, her relationship with God was somewhat different than that of Adam's, not to say she was less important. On the contrary, everything was already completed, before her grand entrance. A very notable aspect was, there was no mention or indication of Eve speaking, before Genesis 3. As mentioned, there are indications of Adam speaking with God in their communion. He also spoke as he identified the animals.

However, the first mention of Eve speaking was not with God nor was it with Adam. The first mention of her speaking was out of order. It was when she spoke to the serpent. Back to Basics, is not an indication that women have no voice? Nevertheless, it is an indication to men and women that we must be careful when we are speaking, to whom we are speaking, and to what we are speaking.

First Lady Eve seems to have set the standard for many women today. It is no secret that women are known for their ability to use their words. Many husbands can testify, as could Adam to this statement. If we go back to Basics and let God do the talking and the building, we could avoid many hurts. First Lady Eve's choice to do the talking caused her husband to lose his job, home, financial stability, and his connection to the CEO of the Universe; she also, lost her sons. Let us get back to the Basics and maintain our positions.

Unless otherwise noted, all biblical passages referenced are from The Holy Bible, Authorized King James Version ®. The New King James Bible: New Testament and Psalms, (Thomas Nelson, Inc, 1994)

The Pit

When you envision your life as God has planned it, your revelation or interpretation can solicit undesirable consequences. What you see may not have happened yet, but you can clearly identify God's plan for you. Your vision will upset people who do not see you in the same way. You also have to be careful to whom you share your vision. If you share it in the wrong season, it will be disregarded and cast down. It is not that what God has revealed is an untruth; it is that you have reveal the truth too soon.

It is sometimes hard to withhold news that makes known your destiny, especially, when you have been viewed as insignificant. You want others to know that you are important to God and his plan. Your reaction and response can be understood and sympathized with, but your exposure can result in unwanted attacks. When people are not ready to see or hear your season, they tend to find unconventional ways to silence you.

They may use character assassination, accusations of incompetence, or even your removal. Transparency is fine when God has given permission. If he has given permission, he will also give protection. There are times and seasons when God will reveal your true purpose. You may be fully aware of your design and God's intentions, concerning your destiny. However, premature delivery will always result in delays, handicaps, and under development. Early delivery can also expose your position to the enemy. Your coming out is in God's time, not yours, thus, restrain yourself. The vision must stay with you for now; the dreams are to help you understand where he is taking you. They are not for sharing, and the scriptural revelations are for an appointed time, as well.

Now if you refuse to wait, concerning your season you may have a Joseph experience. Joseph experienced removal as a result of sharing his dreams. His dreams caused jealousy among his brothers. Although, he was God's chosen his dreams were too big for others to comprehend or embrace. Your call alone will solicit rejection, but the rejection will be much greater when fuel with your dreams.

Eventually, we all will experience the pit. The pit experience will not be long term. Although it will be unpleasant, God will use it to bring you into your purpose. No matter what, you will reach your goal as God has designed. But you must not go to the pit before it is necessary. The times and seasons to walk in your call have been ordained and established by God. Just remember, the pit cannot be avoided it is your path to the Palace.

Use What You Got

Initially, in our faith walk, we often expect perfection. We expect God to make everything brand new; a supernatural makeover is our hope. I know you have heard the sayings; when we came to God, our hands looked new, and our feet did too, but I must say this is not always the case. When starting a new life, many of the same materials and physical elements remain. Why would we throw away the very things that cause us to arrive at our new destination? Of course, there are things that we will never want to be a part of our lives, ever again, but there will be other things, we will need for rebuilding.

Nehemiah did not rebuild the wall with all new materials. He used what he had. He did not allow the conditions of his surroundings nor the conditions of the materials to deter him from the work he had to do. He would not allow the gainsayers, the enemies, nor the attacks to prevent him. The wall had been broken down and burned, but his passion for the people of God and the city remained fortified, in spite of what he had to face. *(Nehemiah 3)*

As you build, beware of *Building Stoppers*. These are those looking for any reason to stop your progress. They will accuse you of code violations, improper materials, and foundational weakness, but do not stop building. Satan will always accuse God's people; it is his job; however, his accusations will not stand. The code violation accusations are only his attempt to get your focus on what is acceptable according to the world's standards. To avoid adjusting your building plans, you will have to build strictly according to God's Blueprint. The improper materials ploy is an attempt to cause you to trade in the Holy things of God and settle for the unclean things of this world.

Finally, there will be an attempt to discredit the foundation on which you are building. The underpinning that you have selected is built on the foundation of the prophets and the apostles, with Christ being the Chief Corner Stone. This foundation consists of the Old Testament and the New Testament. Your bricks and mortar are made of biblical principles that hold it all together.

There are no new materials; there are
only the promises of God. Those promises
are full of the tools needed for the completion
of your wall. God will never allow your
enemies to stop you if you trust him for the
outcome. One thing you can be certain of;
you will not have to build alone.

God promised to be with you giving
you the strength you need to fulfill His plan.
He will provide you with everything you need
to finish the work. You came to this place
with everything required; it will take time and
obedience to develop your spiritual muscles.
If you use what you got, it will be just
enough. The greater one lives in you, so trust
him and build. You got everything you need.

One Size Does Not Fit All

As God's Children, we should know better concerning the diversity of gifts, talents, abilities, and even lifestyles. One size does not fit all. If God were implying in his Word that one size fits all, then what works for one would work for everyone. But one size does not fit all; God has an individualized purpose for each of our lives. We cannot assume that the road that someone takes is the same road we should take, hoping we will have the same results.

Let us consider this as it relates to perception.

One Size Does Not Fit All

- Noah size was eight; only eight human lives were saved on the Ark.

The number of people on the Ark was what God required to replenish the earth. Noah directed his family in alignment with God's commands.

- The Hebrew Boys size was three.
Three was put in the fiery furnace, for
taking a stand for what they believed.
*If you can stand the fire, you will pass the test,
and Jesus will be in the midst of your
situation. Not everybody can go, where God
is sending you. Their presence will cause the
fires to destroy, instead of purification.*
  - The Leopard's size was one. Only one
  returned to show gratitude for his
  healing.
*Will you praise Jesus alone, it only takes one
to set the atmosphere? Can Jesus depend on
you to give him the praise for all the
wondrous things he has done?*

Noah was told to build an ark. He was
also told to warn the people that it was going
to rain. The boat was specifically designed to
carry his size. God knew beforehand what
size would be required. Although he was told
to warn the people, God knew they would
reject him. His size was eight. If he had tried
to fit a bigger size, he would have had to
make room for the extra. As a result of such a
decision, he would have had to remove the
necessary cargo needed to complete the

journey? If we as God's people force fit our purpose, we will lose what it takes to finish the journey successfully.

The Hebrew boy's size was three. Only three in the fiery furnace was needed to motivate the appearance of Jesus Christ. They were dedicated to their call and purpose. A fourth individual without the dedication or persistence would have prevented the intended outcome. Therefore, as God's people, we must understand not everybody can go where he has called us to go. The ten leopards also had a size, and it was one. Although it was a size, ten in the beginning, due to weight loss, only one returned with a grateful heart. Letting go of people that do not fit your destiny will promote a greater move of God in your life.

Size means everything, in the Kingdom, and God has ordained the numbers. Churches are eager to fill their pews, but has God ordained the size. You have filled your pews with dead men. Remember dead men cannot praise or worship. Your size has grown, but your church is dying. Have you gone to the grave to solicit the dead to increase your size? Such, actions will create

divine judgment. When you seek answers
from the dead, there will be consequences.
You might just lose your position. (I Samuel
28:15)

God wants a church that is alive, that is
willing to obey his voice. Do not be hasty
and have the wrong motive in filling the
pews. God said if I am lifted up, I will draw
all men unto me. Therefore, Man/Woman of
God, lift him up with the few that you have,
and he will draw the rest. One size does not
fit all. Be content in the state you are in
because his grace is sufficient. He will send
them. You can draw flies or bees, which do
you want in the church. The difference is
flies are a representation of death, and bees
represent growth and reproduction. What size
are you? God will grow you if you are in
position for growth. Do not step out of
position and miss your blessing.

The Blind Leading the Seeing

I have often read about the blind leading the blind, and they both ended up in a ditch. Oddly, in today's time, I have observed, the blind leading the seeing which, makes no sense. Unfortunately, this is happening right under the noses of the saints. We fail to identify or recognize it because we are responsible for this unorthodox transition-taking place. I know it is a jaw-dropping statement but let me make myself clear. The church has asked the blind to lead, to attract other, blind individuals.

The church wants to be attractive to the world so that they can draw them. To become attractive, we are calling the world to operate in the church. This strategy is very dangerous; it is naturally impossible for the blind to lead the seeing. We are the seeing, we have a vision, and sight to lead those that are lost. We cannot afford to give the blind access to the church; they will only corrupt or contaminate the vision God has given.

Without a vision, the people perish. If we
lose the vision, the church, (the Body of
Christ) will suffer loss.

We must win the blind, not permitting
them to connect sin to righteousness. If we
marry a harlot, we become one with that
harlot. If we are one with a harlot, we are
unclean. Our identification would have
changed due to the connection. Our ability to
affect our environment supernaturally would
be lost. Therefore, we as the Body of Christ
must apply Kingdom Principles to the way we
disciple and win the lost. The basic principles
of winning souls are to follow the command
of Jesus Christ in Matthew 28:19. "Go ye
therefore, and teach all nations, baptizing
them in the name of the Father, and of the
Son, and of the Holy Spirit."

We must restore sight to the blind, not
allowing them to handicap the Body, with
their blindness. Conversion is what God
desire for the lost, not partnership.

The strategy of giving full access to the
blind to attract the outside world is not of
God. They stand in the pulpits, sing in choirs,
lead the music ministry, run auxiliaries, and
they are given the power to counsel our youth.

It is ridiculous. If we read the Word of God correctly, there is no evidence of this type of allowance. It is true they can identify with the lost, but that is about it. They are not Disciples of Christ; they are the very ones that need him. Using the world to do the job of the Church is a lazy approach.

It is our duty as soul winners to do the leg-work. We are to go into the hedges and highways to seek and lead the lost to the kingdom. If we bring leaven into the church, it will infect the unleavened, which will endanger the flock. We cannot afford to lose souls using methods not approved by God. I have been a Christian, for 27 years and have observed what leaven does to a church. I have seen things changed as a result of leaven. The very things rejected became the norm and eventually took over, because a little leaven was allowed. Now it has grown tremendously and has not stopped. Do you remember the old 1958 movie, the Blob? It started with the hand, and it grew until it consumed the entire body. Yes, I have seen the takeover, let us not endanger the Body by placing sickness in the camp.

This strategy may result in a church full of blind individuals including the leaders. Be careful not to lose your sight, collaborating with the blind.

Testimony Break

A Little Leaven

I remember about 25 years ago, attending a very traditional church. The church had a strict dress code. They did not want the women to wear pants, make-up, fancy hairstyles or certain kinds of jewelry. However, as the years past, a family moved into the area from the north. These people were very flashy. They wore pants, lots of make-up and jewelry. The women were attractive; they were very conscious of their appearances. They were singers, ministers, and held various auxiliaries, in the church.

It did not take long at all to see the shifts taking place in the church. The women

begin wearing make-up and pants freely.
Different hairstyles began to surface. It
seemed as though the prayer cloths and other
head coverings were replaced with hair
extensions, wigs, and braids. I must say
things were changing at a fast pace.
Personally, I to, indulged in the new
freedoms, as I learned there were no biblical
restrictions. The changes seem to be affecting
the vast majority.

Unfortunately, the change not only
effected dress code and physical appearances;
there was a change in behavior. It was not
good at all. It seemed as though people were
getting too involved in the outer appearance
and neglected the inner man. When new
things come into the church, it may not be
bad, but we have to be careful as Apostle Paul
said, not to allow our freedoms to become a
stumbling block.

A Blind Church

How did you lose your sight? Why are you stumbling around in darkness? How did you lose your vision? Although, your intentions were pure, and your heart was in the right place, but your plan was flawed. You thought in order to relate to the blind you had to understand their condition. You thought if you could identify with their struggle you could save them. Therefore, you first closed your eyes and pretended to be blind. For a while, you knew what it was like to fall, to make mistakes, and to use a cane to assist your direction. However, that was not enough to grasp a full understanding. It did not give you an in-depth perception, so you decided to pluck out your eyes in hopes that this will be the ultimate condition, providing you with the answers needed to reach the blind. Now your decision has you walking in complete darkness. At this point, you have lost your way and is in need of someone to lead you. There is no way you can spend

limitless time with the lost and not become
stained by the darkness. The question is, are
you tough enough to walk away from those
you love that have the power to pull you
down? Are you tough enough to say I am
okay walking alone? Are you tough enough
to stand alone?

A message to the church: you must not
become what they are. Be not conformed to
the ways of this world but be transformed by
the renewing of your mind. We are the light
of the world, and we have nothing to do with
the darkness. You cannot help others if you
are blind. My late Bishop, William H. Cheek
Sr., would often say to us, "You cannot hang
out with turkeys and soar with eagles." The
Bible says, "Come out from among them be
separated says the Lord and I will receive you
unto myself."

We are different from the world and
winning them to Christ will require Christ-
like character. It is hard to win the lost when
there is no difference between us. They are
the lost coin needing to be discovered. Do not
lose yourself looking. Open your eyes; you
are not blind. Follow the Good Shepherd as

he leads you in the path of righteousness, and
on this path, you will recover your sight.

Answer the Call

Revelation 22:12

And behold, I am coming quickly, and my reward is with me, to give to everyone according to his work. I am the Alpha and Omega, the beginning and the end, the first and the last.

Time is running out people, I got news, breaking news. People of God and people of the world, young and old, time is whining up. It will not be long now. Jesus is at the door. He has given you day after day, week after week, month after month, and year after year. Sadly, to say, you still have not answered the call. Pick up the phone people. You look at your spiritual ID caller, and you ignore the call because you say I am not ready to talk to Jesus. You think, if I talk to him, I will have to stop my mess. I will have to stop back-biting, lying, stealing, and cheating. I have to stop shacking up and sleeping around. I cannot talk to him right now. If I talk to him, he is going to expose my secrets. I am attracted to the same sex, and I do not want anyone to know. I cannot answer this call.

If you answer the call, you will be free from
Satan's control, which has caused you to be a
backbiter, a liar, a thief, a cheater, a
fornicator, and crave for unnatural
relationships.

Listen I have Breaking News; God
wants to set you free, he wants you to turn to
him before it is too late. So, you say what I
do is not so bad. It is not as bad as what
others are doing. Sin is sin and hell is hell. I
want to encourage you to talk to him today.
The Bible says, "When you hear, his voice,
harden not your heart." It is time today to
surrender. Do not let this opportunity slip.
Try to understand this; I was once in the same
place many are in today. But before I could
take my life I answered the call. God saved
me from myself. I did not want to live
anymore. I was only 19 years old and wanted
to end my life.

Yes, it is true I was young, but Satan is
using the same tricks whether you are young
or old. However, I am still fighting every
day. Just because I answered, the call does
not mean I am perfect. I still have to go
through, but now I am not alone. God, fights
with me and for me. He holds things together.
Now ask, yourself the question, why are
things continuing to fall apart, in your life?

No matter how hard you try, things just are
not working out the way you imagined. Well,
you are trying to build a house on sand. No
matter how beautiful or expensive the house
is when the flood comes the house will fall.
If you build your house on the Rock, which is
Jesus Christ, it will stand. Sex outside of
marriage, hiding behind lies, cheating, and
stealing all of it is building on the sand. Your
house will fall because you are backbiting and
cannot admit your struggle with jealousy.

Trust me; you would rather admit your
faults and failures to God, rather than suffer
exposure. Time is running out, and your
secrets are about to be uncovered. Did you
think you were going to keep on keeping on
in your mess? As the old folk says "you just
wrote a check that your hips could not cash."
You are in debt to God. He will drop the
charges if you answer the call. Just because
you are ignoring the call does not eliminate it.
There are just a lot of missed calls, and after a
while, the calls will stop, and you will have
no hope. (Romans 2:5).

It is time to answer the call, follow the
instructions, and live the life that God has
intended. You are living under pretense; you
are not the person you were born to be. God
has your life's blueprint, and he is on the

other end, talk to him and learn your true destiny.

God's GPS

You may say to yourself; I thought this was the place, where there would be no more struggles. I thought; I could finally rest. Well, this is the place where the greater works will be manifested. This is also the place, where you will have to fight. If the Israelites encountered giants, so will you. You will have to stand up to your giants. You must make your declaration, that God is the only God, and then take their heads. What made you think, you would not have to fight for what was yours?

It is the only way to possess the land. The Israelites had to physically, take the land even though God had already given it to them. Their enemies inhabited their possession. There will be times in your life that you will have to put up a fight to get what is yours. As you are fighting, do not think for one moment the enemy is going to step back and do nothing about your stepping into another level, a new dimension, and possessing what was promised to you.

Your new level will accompany a new anointing, more power, and a new position. How bad do you want the thing God has promised to you? If you trust him, he will bring you out of Egypt and into a land flowing with milk and honey. Once you realize, without Him you can do nothing, you will be on your way, and your GPS will be set (God's Perfect Salvation). The GPS will now provide you with vital information required to reach your destination.

GPS will provide the Time (St. John 9:4)

I must work the works of him that sent me, while it is day: the night cometh when no man can work. On this path, you must be mindful of the time. Although we are on the journey to the Promised Land, we must not forget the work that must be done in the process. We are examples to the world; we must represent Christ on the journey. We spend too much time playing church, following the program and enforcing business as usual. We have to get with God's program and be about our Father's business.

We may not all arrive in our promised land at the same time, because of our positions. Some are just coming out of Egypt, others are coming out of the wilderness, and there are those that are taking the city of

Jericho. But if we trust and believe God, we will arrive at our destination.

Yes, it is true; we may be approaching the Promised Land at different times as it relates to our positions. For this very reason, we will need a GPS to lead us in the right direction and keep us on schedule. No man knows the day or the hour when the Son of God shall come. Stay on the path and be ready for his return. Time is running out.

GPS will provide the Distance (Job 24:13)

"There are those who rebel against the light, who do not know its ways or stay in its paths. In this journey your path will consist of various obstacles, however, if you walk in the light, as he is in the light, you have fellowship with one another, and the blood of Jesus, his Son, purifies you from all sin." (NIV) If you go the distance, you will find that you are never alone on the path because the Shepherd is leading you. Be not weary in well doing for you shall reap if you faint not.

GPS will provide the Routes (Psalms 23:4)

Even though I walk through the darkest valley, I will fear no evil, for you are with me;

your rod and your staff, they comfort me.
(NIV)

Your routes to the Promised Land will not be smooth, attractive, or desirable but you must know that God promised that he would never leave you nor forsake you. The journey to the Promised Land prepares you for the promises. Do not regret the route or the hardship; it's working for your good. Your Damascus road is leading you to your destiny. Although, you may temporarily lose your sight during the journey, trust God to be a light to your feet and a lamp to your pathway.

GPS will make you aware of the Tolls

On this journey to the Promised Land, you will soon realize that there are tolls that must be paid. There had to be a price paid for you to access this path and take this journey. However, it will cost you nothing because blood was shed and life was given, that you could have access. Jesus Christ, the Son of the Living God, gave his life that you could choose this path. You have a choice to trust the leading of the shepherd. His death, burial, and resurrection provided the strength you need to finish the race that has been set before you.

GPS will report all The Accidents

Although you have chosen this journey
and have gained access to the Promised Land,
there will be mistakes, and you will fall short
of the glory of God. However, you have to
remember Jesus Christ is our living hope he
has redeemed us from death to life. No longer
do we have to dwell on failures or past sins
because (Micah 7:19) says *He will turn again,
he will have compassion upon us; he will
subdue our iniquities, and thou wilt cast all
their sins into the depths of the sea.* There is
forgiveness on this path. So, know and
understand perfection is not a requirement to
enter the Promised Land. His strengths are
made perfect in our weaknesses.

GPS will identify needed Road Work

On this road, you will need to be
restored and replenished. This road is lonely
at times and storms will come. But there is no
need for pit stops; He has the power to
provide what you need, while you continue to
press towards the mark of a higher calling.
He will work in you, both to will and, to do of
his good pleasures. Be confident of this very

thing, that he who hath begun a good work in you will perform *it* until the day of Jesus Christ: This is how you get to the promise land; follow the GPS (God's Perfect Salvation). He is the Way, the Truth, and the Life. No one comes to the Father except through Jesus Christ, and he is God's Perfect Salvation. His sheep know his voice and a stranger they will not follow. Follow the king to the kingdom.

You have reached your destination: Now that you have arrived, please do not expect to observe the promises with your natural eye. You cannot see your next level; you cannot see your deliverance or healing, you cannot see the kingdom. Those things seen are temporary, but the unseen things are eternal. Your level is eternal; your healing is eternal, and his kingdom is eternal.
The coming of the kingdom of God is not something that can be observed, nor will people say, 'Here it is,' or 'there it is,' because the kingdom of God is in you." Your relationship with the Lord, as you travel on this journey will have developed even more as you walk in obedience to the instructions of the GPS (God's Perfect Salvation).

Your New Level and Dimension are where you will experience an abundant life. The Promised Land is within you. Your healing is in the Promised Land; your restoration is in the Promised Land, your prosperity is in the Promised Land, your husband/wife is in the Promised Land, everything you need to be successful in the kingdom, is located in the promise land.

Today, let us take steps that will lead us to the promise land. Let us make conscious decisions that will give us a clear direction. GPS (God's Perfect Salvation) will always lead us to a higher level. Today we have received the GPS's instructions, which gives directions to the promise land. Now, are you ready to start this journey?

Conversion Testimony
In God's Hands Now

In 1990, I found myself alone and broken with a newborn baby, as a single mom. Before salvation, my life was riddled with abuse, brokenness, and hopelessness. It did not seem so bad back then because I did not know much of what Jesus had to offer. I remember sitting in front of the television, one late night after my family had fallen asleep. I was listening to a Tele-Evangelist speaking, he said reach your hand out if you believe and touch the screen, I was probably in high school at the time. I did what he asked, and nothing happened. I wanted so badly for something to change my life.

My life had taken a turn for the worst, after high school, and after dropping out of college. I became suicidal. I tried to think of ways to take my life that would be painless and would not account for self-murder. My life was truly miserable, and I was at the lowest point of all times. When I stop concentrating on death, I began walking in crippling fear. I was unable to leave the house most days because fear gripped me to the core. I began to see and hear things literally.

I remember during this time, walking from the market and hearing footsteps behind me, crunching through the fallen leaves. The steps were very clear and distinct, but when I turn there was no one there, but it felt like someone was there watching me. I saw figures standing in my home, and I was afraid to leave my room, because of what I had seen. I felt as though I was suffocating.

Finally, the night of November 28, 1990, this was the last time this entity would be able to cripple me with fear. It manifested and stood behind me as I held my two-week-old daughter in my arms. She turned her small head and began to stare at what stood behind us. I was too afraid to turn to see what stood so close to my child and I. That night I was reading the New Testament although I did not understand it, I felt reading it would protect me. I cried bitterly after reading about Jesus's sufferings and crucifixion, as I cried, I could sense the presence of something evil. I built up enough nerve to turn, and when I did, it was no longer there.

At this point, I realized I needed Jesus. I received him that night. I remembered there was one real person I knew that loved the Lord and loved me, and she was a phone call away. She was a minister who took me to church with her when I was fifteen years old. I had not spoken to this person in a long time, but on this night of fear and brokenness, the very Bible, I held in my hand had her phone number in it. I called her, and she led me to the Lord as I kneel by my bedside at 20 years old. This was the night my life would change forever. I made the call and gave my life to Christ. Fear was Satan's last ploy to keep me from God.

The biggest change I have noticed in my life is that God has given me power over the enemy. I do not have to be afraid anymore. He has given me a new lease on life, and it was free of charge. God has given me a freedom that I have never experienced before. Once my life began to change, I noticed that things that once bothered me, and got me down no longer had the power to

burden me. I cannot imagine my life without
Jesus. I cannot live without him. I love life,
and I want to live every day giving my life
back to the Lord. I did not understand before,
why he would die for me, but now that I do, I
owe him everything.

When I decided to give my life to the
Lord, I was determined to share this with
everyone. My family saw the change in me,
and the change opened their eyes to God's
love. The biggest changes in my life have
affected my friends and loved ones. I have
won them to Christ because of Jesus' love. I
have allowed the Lord to make changes in
me. I realized if I surrender to his love and
forgiveness, I would have a testimony to share
with others so that they can do the same.

A Little Faith

I wonder sometimes do people know it takes faith to praise God. When you praise God, you are saying to the natural and supernatural world, I believe in the God of Heaven and Earth, the one, and only true and living God. You are announcing to everything in the earth that my God is real. God inhabits the praises of His people; your praise announces his power and majesty. However, when you enter into his Gates unthankful and his courts with complaints, there are no blessings for you. He deserves the praise, and he deserves to be recognized. The release of your blessings is activated by your faith and your praise.

Galatians 3:6
Abraham believed God, and it was accounted to him for righteousness. Know ye therefore that they which are of faith, the same are the children of Abraham.

Psalms 67:1- 6
God be merciful unto us, and bless us, and
cause his face to shine upon us; Selah. Then
shall the earth yield her increase; and God,
even our own God, shall bless us. (KJV)
Many times, when we are talking about
faith, we have to remind ourselves as
believers that we have been given a measure
of faith. This measure was utilized when we
received salvation. Every believer has a level
of faith based on the substance of things, they
hope. Guess what; the sinner has faith too.
Roman 12:3, God has given a measure faith
to all men. However, there is a difference the
children of faith eat from the table, everybody
else begs for the crumbs. *Matt. 15:26, But*
Jesus replied, "It is not right to take the
children's bread and toss it to the dogs.
(KJV)
So, the question is what is your level of
faith or what is it that you hope for? What do
you believe? What do you hold as truth?
Does your level of faith determine your
closeness to God the father? Well, the
disciples walked with Jesus, ate with Jesus,
and communed with Jesus, but at times were

rebuked because of their little faith, but their fellowship stayed in tack.

Matthew 6:30
Wherefore, if God so clothes the grass of the field which today is, and tomorrow is cast into the oven shall he not clothe you, O ye of little faith. (KJV)

Matthew 8:26
And he said unto them, Why are you fearful, O ye of little faith? Then he arose and rebuked the winds and the sea, and there was a great calm.

He does not leave you, but he sends fires that will try your faith. The trying of your faith is more precious than gold.

The three Hebrew boys', faith, prevented them from bowing down or eating the king's meat. Although they did the right thing in pleasing God, they were still put in the fiery furnace, and its degrees was increased, but they did not fret themselves. There will be times in our lives as believers that our faith has to be taken to the next level. The three Hebrew boys believed that God was going to handle their situation, and as a result of their faith, Jesus showed up right on time. See, we have to stay in the fire and not come out until we see Jesus. Are you tough enough?

Recognize that your faith is not just for you, it is for the unbelievers. Many that were looking at the three boys in the fire also saw Jesus, and the boys came out with no smell of smoke or burns. This caused them to believe. Is your degree of faith able to transform the sinner? Is your degree of faith able to keep you from looking like what you have been through?

Hebrews chapter eleven tells us all about faith. *Hebrews 11:1, "Now faith is the substance of things hoped for the evidence of things not seen." (KJV)*

On this journey of understanding faith and its importance, we will soon realize that God has left a legacy of believers to solidify the rewards of having faith. These were the patriarchs of faith.

Look at the degree of faith that you see in **Abel** as he offers up a greater sacrifice than Cain does. His faith is still speaking to us today, reminding us to give our best.

Enoch demonstrated a degree of faith that caused him to be transformed from the natural to the supernatural, which left a testimony that he pleased God; **Noah** had a degree of faith that caused him to build an Ark believing that it was going to rain when it had never rain before. <u>However, God said it, and he believed.</u> He built the ark, collected his family, the animals, and shut the door and waited. Sometimes, when you believe God to move you have to be still and wait, the rain is coming. Learn to be still. Noah faith saved his family and started a new civilization. Noah became an heir of righteousness because he believed God.

Look at **Abraham's** faith; his faith made him the father of many nations, and a friend of God. He believed and trusted in him. He was called to go to Canaan, which was the Promised Land to the people of God. He did not waver, but instead, he packed up, moved his family, and relocated, believing God. He did not know where he was going, but he trusted the leading of God. Sara also benefited from his faith, God opened her womb, and she had a son at an old age.

Just a little Faith

- Jacob faith allowed him to fight with an angel for a blessing from the Lord
- Joseph faith took him from the pit to the palace and brought his family into the blessings of prosperity
- Ester was married to the king and gained his favor. Her faith saved the nation of Israel from death.
- Ruth's faith caused her to marry a good husband, who was in the bloodline of Jesus Christ.
- Joshua's faith got him and the Israelites across the Jordan into the Promised Land
- David's faith killed a giant, made him king, and established his throne forever.
- Ezekiel by faith spoke and prophesied to the dry bones. Who was the whole house of Israel, exiled from their land 70 years. His faith resurrected their hope, and they were able to return to their land, believing and trusting in their God.

Now Isaiah is asking us today, whose report do we believe. Your faith can speak after you

are dead and gone, your faith can translate
you from this life to eternal life, your faith can
rise above the storm and save your family,
and your faith says age is nothing but a
number, you can give birth to the promises of
God. Your faith can take you to unfamiliar
territory and make you great. The question
remains, whose report do you believe? His
report says you are free; his report says you
are healed, his report says you have the
victory. I believe the report of the Lord.

Often as believers, we have accepted a
life beneath our privileged positions, and it is
because of little faith. All you need is faith
the size of a mustard seed. With faith that
small, you can remove a mountain from its
place and cast it into the sea.
What mountain in your life needs to be
removed? What situations in your life have
been lingering year after year with no
solution? The removal of the mountain is in
your mouth. The bible says that life and death
are in the power of the tongue. We must have
faith to speak; we must have the faith to
declare and decree that the mountain gets out
of our way.

You may think that moving a mountain is impossible, but that which is impossible to man is possible to God, and he has equipped you with what you need to move what is blocking your spiritual blessings.

I want to reassure you that all you need is a little faith. The same size faith it took for you to believe for your salvation is the same amount of faith you need to be healed, to be set free, to prosper financially, and to have a healthy relationship. As people of, God we give up too fast. Wait I say on the Lord, and he shall renew your strength. You shall mount up with wings like eagles, you will run and not get weary, and you will walk and not faint. Your faith will cause you and others to overcome.

I remember as a little girl about eight years old; I really didn't know much about God, Jesus, or the Bible. I do remember my grandmother on her knees praying, and I was upset, thinking it was cruel that she had to stay down there so long, at her age. But let me tell you, her faith is why I stand before many, and share my stories. Now, I am the one that stays on my knees, often all night.

The mountain that the devil had placed in front of her children and grandchildren has been moved. My grandmother had passed away a long time before, I surrendered to the Lord, but just like Abel, her prayers could still be heard. The substance of her <u>*now faith*</u> was her children and grandchildren, she died before the evidence was revealed, but she died believing.

I was the first in my family to give my life to Christ. I believed God for my mother, and she surrendered, she and I believed for my stepfather, and he became an awesome man of God. I also have brothers and sisters that have given their lives to Christ. I believed my grandmother learned how to pray in her most holy faith, praying in the Holy Ghost. Therefore, the levels of faith are not measured in size, but degrees, Little Faith, Weak Faith, Great Faith, Genuine Faith, Holy Faith and, Unwavering Faith.

Faith is not only, what you believe; it is what you do. Faith without works is dead. You have to do something. It takes faith to work a job full of demons; it takes faith to raise your children as a single parent, it takes faith to keep on keeping on when people talk about you, making false accusations about you. It took faith for Moses to lift up his staff, point it toward the Red Sea and cross on dry ground. The greater One lives within you and you can do all things through Christ who strengthens you.

When you activate, the mustard seed, mountains will start moving. Weak faith becomes strong, little faith becomes great, wavering faith becomes unwavering. You may not see it all happen in your lifetime, but your little faith puts it all in motion. So, do not be discouraged with a little faith, it is all you need to make the impossible possible, it's all you need to open closed doors, it is all you need to lay hands on the sick and see them recover. You can do all things through Christ; all you need is a little faith.

You Need a Lesson Plan

Did you know, to walk in the will of God, you would need a lesson plan? Often we go about our business doing whatever comes. But you need to know if you are to please God you must follow His plan. As you follow his plan you will soon realize, there are lessons involved. God wants his people to learn how to follow his instructions. In the natural classroom, certain things are required to reach the students.

The number one thing that is needed is a teacher that understands the curriculum. The teacher must have the ability to teach what he or she knows. To impart truth, one must know the truth. In my classroom, I must have a lesson plan to cover certain areas of my content weekly. I have an academic blueprint that I use to teach during a certain period, for a certain amount of days, which is referred to as a pacing guide. I also implement a word wall that covers the vocabulary related to particular content. I use visual resources, hands-on resources, group, and individual activities, but none of this would work if I had no understanding, of the content. Having said and shared that, I want you to understand, the importance of having a plan.

God has a lesson plan, he used, his Word to instruct the children of Israel in the form of two stone tablets. God uses activities such as, prayer meetings, individual activities that motivates prayer, meditation, and fasting. Just as the students, learn differently in the classroom, so does God's students (children). There are different levels of growth and understanding, however, the more you study, the better understanding that will be obtained. We must take heed of God's plan. Do not try to go at it without a plan. Follow the plan and move to the next level. Each level will require a new lesson plan. Do not try to slack in any areas or rush through it, if so you will find yourself repeating the process.

The Bible is a Lesson Plan

➢ (The Word) Wall
➢ (Testimonies) Visual Aide
➢ (Assignments) Contains Individual
  Activities
➢ (Corporate Prayer and Worship)
  Contains Group Activities
➢ It contains the Ultimate Graduation
  Plan (Eternal Life) with God

If you desire to graduate on time, the lessons must be learned and applied. It can no longer be a situation, which you only understand the expectations; it has to involve proper implementation. With each lesson, there has to be a demonstration of what has been learned. This will ensure that the assignments have been effective. The demonstration will also reveal your new position, as a teacher. God wants to develop students into effective teachers that can grow the Kingdom. Your growth and development was not for you alone but for those needing the lessons you have learned. It is your testimony that causes you and others to overcome.

Remember:

You can only reach the levels God has intended for you. It is impossible for you to go beyond the boundaries of God's design. You may choose to follow your own path, but your destination will be separation from God. You can only accomplish greater levels by following God's lesson plan.

Your Statement is the Same, Your Punctuation is Different

A statement can be written the same ways repeatedly, but if the punctuation is different the meaning, the urgency, or power of the statement will change. I can change a statement and make it into a question, which may indicate uncertainty or doubt. In the same way as people of God, we must write the vision and make it plain.

The vision that God has put in place is without the need for modification, adjustment, or editing. His words are ever settled. It may not look right to the reader or sound right to the hearer, but without a doubt, it is the Word of God. It is the Plan of God and the vision God has given to his people. The reader of, the Word, the plan, and the vision, will be rejected if presented out of season. Time has a lot to do with this understanding. The vision cannot be altered as a result of its present fit; somethings do not fit until weights are removed. However, the additional weights and sins have prevented comprehension.

Therefore, the question is what kinds of actions are necessary to assist in laying aside the extra.

Well, the vision must remain intact as you move in the things of God. It may seem very unfamiliar to you or out of sorts, but that does not permit you to change the vision in order to fit your perspective. You must lose weights. This will require you to mortify your members, crucify your flesh, and put on the whole armor of God. The flesh wars against the spirit and the spirit wars against the flesh, but if you walk in the Spirit you will not fulfill the lust of human nature. This is an effective weight loss plan.

As weights are laid aside, you will have the ability to stay the course, without altering the directions. God word is forever settled, and it will not change. As you share the Word of God keep every, I dotted and every, T crossed. You have to be tough enough to follow the Lord's instructions for your Life. If you deter and alter the plan, you will be removed.

You Are Tough Enough

Sometimes you may doubt, who you are in Christ. This does not imply that you are not chosen. It is a normal reaction when we take into consideration his perfection. You may wonder why he would want someone like you, with all your issues. You say you will never measure up, and you will always fall short, concerning his expectations. You view yourself as very weak. So why did he choose you?

You are chosen with purpose. God, wants you with all of your imperfections. You are perfect for the job. He wanted someone that needed him. He wanted a child that would love and want him back. Someone he could build up and equipped for the work that must be done. You are a perfect choice. You are tough enough for what he has called you to do.

It does not matter what you have done, what you will do, or what you have not done. God, considered everything about you and concluded that you are the right one for the job. He did not make a mistake. I am sure that there are quite a few who may disagree, but their vote does not count. If you stick to the plan and use what you got, God will use you to build his Kingdom. Are you ready to do what so many have failed in doing? They failed because they stop trusting in the plan, and started to alter the blueprint.

The foundation has been laid, and the laborer has been chosen. Now it is time for the harvest. You have everything that is required to finish this work. Keep your eyes on the prize. Although, you will not get it right every time, understand that God is with you and he will provide you with the tools, and equipment you need to build.

What did you do to deserve such favor, you said, yes? Your yes was the key to the promises of God. Now, the gates are opened, and the flood begins. It is your season and, it is your time. Do not doubt your position. God is in control. God's choice is the right choice. As long as you allow him to do the work through you, you will remain. He called, and you answered. Your obedience will demonstrate to other leaders, ministers,

teachers, husbands, and wives, how to follow
the call.

About the Author

Angela has dedicated her life to fulfilling Gods plans concerning winning the lost to Christ. Writing has been her passion for many years. She uses this tool to reach hearts and homes with her testimonies and purposeful experiences. Through her life, she has had to face tragedy, pains, and failures, but through it, all God has kept her. She writes this book in hopes that the readers will understand that the race is not given to the swift nor the strong, but to the one that endures to the end. Are you strong enough, is not a question related to natural strength, it relates to one's spiritual ability?

She encourages others never to give up in this race. She believes it is our duty to stand, defending the weak, and shattered,

*remembering we were in their shoes not long
ago. As God's hands, Angela writes her life
and experience uniquely and
comprehensively. Her practical application
to staying strong when facing her greatest
weaknesses, derived from her biblical
perspective. The perspective of trusting God
with all her heart and leaning not on her
understanding has given her endurance. She
is strong enough for the season in which she
now stands, prepared to fight the good fight of
faith.*

Are You Tough Enough?

Make a List of your Strengths and Weaknesses.

1.

2.

3.

4.

5.

6.

7.

8.

9.

10.

What do you consider to be a good relationship, based on godly principles?

Who comes first, the church or the family?

How do you build positive connections in order to reach the lost?

When was the last time you led someone to Christ?

Can God trust you with the responsibility of sowing His Word?

Are you in a position to fulfill the Call of God?

Take your list before the Lord in Prayer
Your list can be as long or short as needed.